The Momentum Theorem

The Momentum Theorem

How to Create Unstoppable Momentum in All Areas of Your Life

DAVE RAMSEY

RAMSEY
P R E S S

© 2022 Lampo Licensing, LLC

Published by Ramsey Press, The Lampo Group, LLC
Franklin, Tennessee 37064

Editorial: Jackie Quinn
Cover Design: Chris Carrico and Weylon Smith
Interior Design: PerfecType, Nashville, TN

ISBN: 978-1-942121-75-6

Printed in the United States of America
22 23 24 25 26 POL 5 4 3 2 1

The Momentum Theorem

How to Create Unstoppable Momentum in All Areas of Your Life

Introduction

Have you ever experienced those times when everything you touch seems to turn to gold? Those times when all your ideas are great, and things seem to go right just because things are going right?

That's momentum.

Momentum makes you look smarter and better than you are.

But when you don't have momentum, the opposite is true. You look dumber and worse than you really are. Everything you touch turns to a big pile of crap. Everything that can go wrong does. It feels like you're living in a bad country song.

Until you have momentum, you'll keep looking worse than you really are. Because the work of creating momentum is messy. You'll have mud all over you from clawing and scratching and digging. You'll suffer through false starts and get bruises from blindly bumping into walls and stumbling over roadblocks. But that stuff you're doing—all that dirty, painful, sometimes embarrassing stuff—will likely cause the right things to happen 5, 10, 20 years from now. Things you just can't see yet.

And then one day, it all comes together and you *can* see. In fact, everyone can see. But no one knows how to accurately describe what they're seeing. All the mud is washed off of you, and now you and everything around you looks shiny. So assumptions are made. The process of how you got to this place is overlooked, and the spotlight shines only on the sparkling results. And just like that, you're mistakenly deemed an *overnight success.*

Really? *Overnight success?* I mean, shut up.

I've laughed at the idea of *overnight success* for years. At several points in my career, people tried to categorize me and the growth of my company, Ramsey Solutions, as an *overnight success.* On the surface, it makes for a much more exciting story. We as a culture seem to celebrate the drama and intrigue of such things. But I've done enough stupid to know that *overnight* and *on the surface* are too short and shallow to produce anything with momentum and meaning. It takes getting in the trenches with people over the long haul, scratching and clawing in the dark, to even get a peek at the edge of daylight. And often, it takes digging yourself out of your own trench first.

No, it's not sexy. I may have even lost some readers at the word *trench,* and that's okay. Creating momentum isn't for everyone. Not everyone's ready to go to the next level of living. Some will never turn the dial. They'll never know how exhilarating and rewarding shifting to the next gear can be.

But you're still reading. That tells me you're hungry—or at least curious. Or maybe you're just plain sick and tired of being stuck on dry and dusty dead-end roads. You've allowed a dark corner of your tired brain and maybe even a sliver of your thirsty soul to wonder what it would be like to experience just a little bit of momentum. You've wondered, *How do I even get momentum? What would that possibly look like in my life—my business, my leadership, my marriage, my parenting, my health, my faith, my finances?*

Funny, I didn't wonder about these things until I was actually experiencing momentum. My head had been down for years, just grinding away at the next thing in front of me. Until I looked up one day and realized I was smack-dab in the middle of it. I guess that's why some people mistake momentum as *overnight success*. Just like those around me, I didn't know what to call it at the time, but it felt like an incredible phenomenon way beyond me and my own efforts. And I wanted more of it.

So I went about trying to analyze momentum so I could define it and experience it more deliberately and more often. I looked back at the course of actions and events that had propelled me to that moment. I studied my story—all the mountain-top highs and ocean-bottom lows—to determine the what, the why, and the how.

What emerged was, of all things, a theorem. A mathematical formula of sorts—not so much about numbers but principles. (Think *theory of gravity*, even though I'm by far no Einstein. Our hairstyles alone should tell you that!)

I call it The Momentum Theorem. And it blows the notion of *overnight success* out of the water. It's a theorem that explains how, when you focus and spend some time digging and planting in trenches *and* you invite God into your efforts, amazing things can happen. Not here-today-gone-tomorrow things. Lasting, life-changing, unstoppable things.

And the most exciting part? The Momentum Theorem isn't just for me. Anyone can apply its principles and create unstoppable momentum in their lives. Today, that anyone is you.

In the pages ahead, I'll break down the elements of the equation for you and illustrate each one by sharing stories from my journey. As you read, think about your own story. Think about the areas of your life where you most need momentum. What parts are stuck and need a big boost of mojo? What muddy trench are you slogging in? Where do you just need something to break wide open?

Now, let's get started. First, we'll jump into a couple of trenches I've been in to see what *overnight success* really looks like . . .

The First Trench

I heard the agony in my wife Sharon's voice on the other end of the phone. I tried to offer her some reassuring words, but I knew words alone wouldn't patch the wound. I promised I'd be there soon, then hung up and raced home from the office. Hot anger pulsed through my veins as I drove. I walked in the kitchen and saw Sharon sitting in tears at our old oak table. The bills stacked high next to the old rotary phone told the suffocating story. She had just taken the bajil-lionth call from another nasty collector, and this one had gone for the jugular.

Barreling toward bankruptcy, we had both taken our share of snide calls from chumps in cheap suits demanding money we didn't have. But this time, the jerk took it too far and made it personal. Feeling big and mighty from several states away at the other end of the phone line, *this* guy badgered Sharon about our finances and then dared to ask her why she was even married to a loser like me who couldn't pay his bills. Instead of *professionally* discussing the amount due and arranging for a *reasonable* way to collect it, he had the audacity to attack our marriage—the one thing holding on by a thread in our crumbling house of cards.

This and several more excruciating moments like it are only snapshots of the deep trench Sharon and I had to climb out of in the late '80s. At that time, things like *focus* and *momentum* didn't even cross my mind. *Survival* was the only thing I could think about. And Ramsey Solutions? Not even a blip on the radar yet.

The Fall

I started from nothing but a hard work ethic and an entrepreneurial spirit in overdrive. By the time I was 26, I had a net worth of a little over a million dollars. I was making $250,000 a year. That's more than $20,000 a month net taxable income. I was really having fun. But 98 percent truth is still a lie. And that remaining 2 percent can cause big problems, especially with $4 million in real estate. The truth was, $3 million of the $4 million was tied up in short-term loans. That's a lot of debt to be on the hook for. And I'm the idiot who signed up for it.

When the bank I took the loans from was sold to another bank, they called all my notes at once. Over the course of the next two and a half years, with a marriage gasping for air and both a brand-new baby and a toddler in tow, I lost everything and finally declared bankruptcy.

Cue the thunderous thud at the bottom of the first trench.

The Climb

Maybe you've heard the saying, "There's no place to go but up." It's true (unless playing victim and staying paralyzed in dark places is your thing). I realized I could choose to throw a life-long pity party and stay where I was or I could start scratching, clawing, and climbing my way out. I chose to climb.

I started looking for sturdy footholds. I got ultra-focused about learning how money really works, how I could take control of it, and how I could manage it with confidence. I stopped taking advice from broke people and read everything I could get my hands on. I interviewed older rich people—people who made money and *kept* it. I came to realize that my money problems largely began and ended with the person in my mirror. If I could learn to manage the character I shaved with every morning, I would win with money.

Most importantly, I got to know God during this time and what His Word says about handling money. Turns out, He's got a lot to say about how we should steward the gifts He's given us. As I grew in my relationship with Him, it became clear to me that the trench I was learning to climb out of wasn't just about *me*. It was part of my path to helping *others* climb out of theirs.

The Second Trench

Most people who make it out of a trench don't turn around and jump back into another. But once I got to the top of mine and could finally see daylight, I looked back and saw so many people—millions of them—stuck in the same hole I'd just fought my way out of. I knew their pain and their hopelessness. And I knew I had to jump back in, share what I'd learned, and climb shoulder to shoulder with them. That's the funny thing about hope. Once you experience it, you can't help but want everyone to experience it in their own lives.

So in 1992, I formed a company that would later become Ramsey Solutions. I wanted to bring hope and help to folks who were struggling financially and to folks who were looking for a way to avoid financial struggle altogether. I developed and began to teach the 7 Baby Steps that lead to financial peace. I spent hours upon hours counseling people on all the things Sharon and I had learned the hard way—how to budget, get out of debt, save, invest, and give generously. Based on these principles, I wrote and self-published the book *Financial Peace* and began selling it out of my car. With a friend of mine, I also started a local radio call-in show called *The Money Game* (now known as *The Ramsey Show*). It wasn't long before both the book and the radio show took off.

Financial Peace became the number one-selling book in the state of Tennessee. Soon after, a literary agent called me and told me I needed to sell it to a publisher in New York who was willing to give me a lot of money for it. I may have self-published, but I knew the difference between having margin and having royalties. Margin was bigger and better. So I told her, "Thanks, but they don't have enough money to buy this book. They should've bought it when it was in the trunk of my car. Now we've sold 150,000 copies."

She insisted that I at least let the publisher come and talk to me. She tried to convince me that a deal with them could take *Financial Peace* to another level I just wouldn't be able to reach by myself. I thought, *Yeah, you're an agent. That's what you all say.* But instead I said, "Yeah, y'all can come down and talk, but unless you bring a Brinks truck, I really don't think you'll have enough money to buy this book." Turns out, they did.

I signed with Viking Press, and they *did* do stuff I had never imagined. I went on a 21-city book tour. Before I knew it, *People* magazine picked up our story. Then I was interviewing with Matt Lauer on *The Today Show*. Next came appearances on *The 700 Club*, *Sally Jessy Raphael*, CNN, and *CBS This Morning*. And then . . . *Financial Peace* hit the *New York Times* bestseller list.

I can't say that I had my head around it at this point, but I just had a sense that something big was going on. I started thinking, *Where could all of this possibly go from here?* I mean, even to me, it started feeling like just yesterday I had written a little self-published book and I was doing a little hillbilly radio show on a handful of regional stations. But now it seemed like there was this undeniable undercurrent moving me forward. And then, just like the agent had said, the buzz reached *another level.* The queen bee herself was interested in having me on her show.

Oprah

In those days, being on *The Oprah Winfrey Show* was like magic dust for any author. If you could get on *Oprah*—BOOM!—your book went straight to number one. She seemed to have unbelievable power. Publishers and publicists worshiped at her feet.

So you can imagine my excitement with *Financial Peace* hovering around the number two and three spots on the *New York Times* bestseller list! My team and I knew an interview with Oprah could take it to number one. But there was another new financial book on the scene. Suze Orman had released a financial book the same day that *Financial Peace* had come out. We were watching it but weren't too concerned because, at that time, it wasn't high on the *Times* list.

And then—Suze got on *Oprah*. Just like magic, she sold millions in the next 60 days and left me in the dust. (Not quite how I had pictured Oprah's magic dust working.)

But all was not lost. Oprah's people called us too. And called and called and called. They'd call and tease my team that they'd like to have me on the show. We'd discuss possible interview topics and specific story ideas, and then the calls would stop. This happened so much that our joke got to be: We're the people that have *almost* been on *Oprah* more than anybody!

This back and forth went on for years. Meanwhile, we launched a new book called *The Total Money Makeover*, which went to number one on the bestseller lists. We were working like crazy. I was doing interviews on all the top-rated shows and huge live events all over the nation.

Around this time, Lesley Stahl's team called from *60 Minutes* and they were interested in doing a piece with us too. Lesley came to Tennessee and captured all kinds of footage: interviews with me, highlights of our day-to-day work and our fans' powerful stories. They ran the piece that October, and the reaction to it nearly blew up our servers! It was awesome.

Finally, Oprah's team called again, and we actually did the taping that spring. Even though we didn't have an official air date, Oprah's team told us they would air our segment sometime the following May. It seemed like everything was coming together. All the major bookstores loaded up on copies of *The Total Money Makeover* so they'd have enough in stock when the story aired. Then Oprah's team changed their minds *again* and told us they liked our particular segment so much that they wanted to air it in September because that's when they draw their largest audiences and advertisers. We were hopeful, but let's just say, we weren't holding our breath.

About that time, *60 Minutes* called and said our show had been their highest-rated show the prior year, and they wanted to rerun it in August. Praying our *Oprah* segment would actually run in September, we asked if *60 Minutes* would run their piece at the *end* of August. They did. And shockingly enough, Oprah's crew finally did run our segment in September! After all that waiting, we "all of a sudden" had incredible media momentum from our back-to-back *60 Minutes* and *Oprah* hits.

Books were selling like wildfire. More big interviews came with Larry King and regular appearances on Fox. Things were rockin' and rollin' around Ramsey Solutions. It was exciting. Maybe too exciting. All the hype made it easy for the outside world and even our team to start believing we were an overnight success. And that just didn't sit right in my soul.

Remember, momentum makes you look smarter and better than you are. I knew that this "*Oprah/60 Minutes* effect" wasn't lightning in a bottle or some random event. And it sure as heck wasn't an overnight phenomenon! This moment was 20 years in the making. I had declared bankruptcy in 1988. I self-published *Financial Peace* in 1992. I landed on *Oprah* in 2005. And all along the way, my team and I had been in the trenches. We'd been to the muddy bottom and worked our butts off day after day to help hundreds of thousands of people get out of the trenches too.

Sure, it was wonderful, and we were thankful for the lift Oprah and all the other publicity brought to our business. But none of it was our salvation. God was and is. Our blessings come from Him. The publicity just accentuated all the digging and planting that we had done and that God had blessed. It put an exclamation point on all the blood, sweat, and tears that had gotten us to this moment. No, this wasn't random at all. This was harvest time in fields that I knew would continue to grow and produce as long as we had focus and faith.

I just needed a way to capture for my team the essence of what was happening. A way to tell the *whole* story, not just a shiny part.

A way to help them see everything it really takes to build and keep momentum. And that's how The Momentum Theorem came to be:

$$Fi/T(G) = M$$

Focused Intensity, over Time, multiplied by God,
equals Unstoppable Momentum.

It's been an operating business principle at Ramsey Solutions ever since. But The Momentum Theorem is much more than a business principle. It's a life principle. And it's not exclusive to my story. It can be a part of your story too. No matter if you've been in a trench or two, you're at the bottom of one right now, or you're right in the middle of exciting growth you can't explain, understanding and applying the elements of The Momentum Theorem can help you move the needle in any area of your life. Let's dig in to each element of the equation and see how.

The Momentum Theorem Explained

Have you ever had *good* barbeque? I'm talking the kind that makes the angels sing and the neighbor's dog howl *good*. Well, anyone who knows *good* barbeque knows that it's been cooked low and slow for days. Momentum is like *good* barbeque: cooked slow and steady, not microwaved. It's that same low and slow, concentrated effort that best characterizes the elements of The Momentum Theorem. First, *F* for *Focus*.

F for *Focus*

Sadly, almost no one in our current culture can stay focused anymore. The pitiful fact that we can now order barbeque in a fast-food drive-thru tells us that! We don't know what a low and slow simmer is. We're into microwaves, not crockpots.

The truth is, since mobile internet came on the scene, our attention spans have shrunk. One study even claims that the attention span of the average adult is now only eight seconds—less than that of a goldfish! I'm not sure how you quantify the attention span of a goldfish, but I do know it's hard for most people to watch a television show all the way through without changing the channel or picking up their phones and getting sucked down one of a million rabbit holes. We just can't keep our minds on anything. Which means we can't stay with a task long enough to actually become good at it. The days of apprenticing something for 10 years to become a professional are gone. Everyone wants a genie in a bottle.

Barriers to Focus

So, what causes us to lose our focus? There are probably as many factors as there are personality types, but the story I'm about to share narrows it down to two underlying reasons.

Several years ago, I was speaking at a rookie camp for the Tennessee Titans. My task was to teach money principles to these young pro athletes and explain to them that NFL really stands for *Not For Long*. At that time, the average NFL career across all positions lasted only 2.6 years. Not only that, but it was reported that just two years after they retired, 78 percent of former NFL players went bankrupt or were under financial stress. To make matters worse, the divorce rate among these guys was estimated between 60 and 80 percent. See what I mean? *Not. For. Long.* From every angle, it seemed the odds were stacked against pro football players. But at this particular event, I did my best to give these rookies hope. I encouraged them to follow the Baby Steps plan with the same amount of discipline and focus that they apply to their game. Only then, I told them, would they beat the odds.

While I was speaking, I noticed a veteran player leaning against the back wall, listening. I recognized him as a Hall of Fame wide receiver. Afterward, he complimented me on my talk. "That was really good, Dave. You're right, they have to learn how to focus. If you're going to win at anything, you've got to focus."

I thanked him and then asked him a burning question that has always frustrated me as a football fan. "Speaking of focus, can I ask you an uncomfortable question? I've just got to know. How is it that, as a wide receiver, you've basically done one thing since you were seven years old—catch a football—and yet you can be standing in the end zone by yourself, the quarterback throws a tight spiral, it hits you right in the numbers, and you drop the ball?"

He smiled as I gulped, suddenly realizing the size of his massive frame next to my not-as-massive frame and the critical-sounding words I had just blurted out. And you'd think I would stop there, right? But for some reason, my mouth just kept running . . . "I mean, you're in the top one-tenth of 1 percent of athletes in the entire freaking world, and all you gotta do is catch a football. You're paid $10 million to do that one thing . . . and you still drop the ball. How is that possible?"

The train had left the station. There was no taking back the word vomit. Bracing for impact, I held my breath and waited for his response.

He smiled again. I got the feeling he'd been asked this before. He said, "It's easy. Assuming the ball is catchable—that it was thrown within arm's reach and didn't require some kind of acrobatic maneuver to snag—wide receivers at the pro level only lose focus and drop the ball for one of two reasons: fear or greed."

Fear

"What do you mean?" I asked, silently thanking God Almighty that he had understood the sincere curiosity behind my unfiltered line of questioning.

"Well," the player said, "you've probably heard television announcers describe this by saying, 'He heard footsteps.' What that really means is, a Sasquatch the size of a car is getting ready to break my butt in half, and whether I catch the ball or not, I'm going to be in an ice bath for three days after he hits me. It means I can *hear* and *feel* him coming—hear his actual footsteps and feel physical terror running through my entire body."

I gulped again.

"The longer you've been doing this," he said, "the more you know how bad it's going to hurt. And the fear of the pain can ultimately cause you to lose focus."

Even though I've never been physically pummeled by a Sasquatch wearing a helmet and running at full speed, I know the emotional equivalent of the fear he was talking about. I'm willing to bet *you* know it too. We've *all* been bulldozed by something hard in life, and we fear it happening again. It causes us to lose focus and not complete the play right in front of us. We take our eyes off the ball because we'd rather avoid hard things. But fearing pain and all the worst-case scenarios only paralyzes us, preventing us from taking action. And ultimately, it keeps us from scoring touchdowns in our work and our life.

Greed

Greed, on the other hand, works the opposite way. It doesn't paralyze us from taking action. It actually causes us to lose focus by taking the *wrong* action.

The wise Hall of Famer went on to explain . . . "Picture a wide receiver with nothing between him and the end zone. All the receiver has to do is catch the ball, turn, and run 15 yards into touchdown territory. But instead, he lets his mind run faster than his feet. While the ball is spiraling through the air, he's imagining himself doing his touchdown dance in front of 80,000 people. In his mind, he's already spiking the ball, doing the Funky Chicken, and making the top play of the day on *SportsCenter*."

"He gets greedy," I said.

"Yes, he gets greedy." The player nodded and sighed as if he'd seen it happen millions of times in his career. "He doesn't see the ball all the way in and finish the job. Instead, he starts thinking, *I've got this. This one's mine. I've worked hard and this is my moment.* He glances at the end zone where the party will begin, and all of a sudden the ball hits him in the chest and falls to the ground. In a nanosecond, greed has stolen his points and his glory."

The scene this veteran player described sounded familiar to me. I'd seen it play out not just on a football field but in life *and* in business. Smart, talented, genuinely good people get ahead of themselves. They get their eyes fixed on the end zone before they've even caught the ball. Instead of doing the work, they skip important steps and jump straight to the rewards. They learn the hard way that greed is a liar and a thief. Greed tells you that you're entitled to things you've haven't worked for or earned. Greed robs you of self-awareness and humility and causes you to lose more than focus. It causes you to lose respect.

The football analogies my Hall of Famer friend shared with me that day are powerful. They show us just how important focus is—and how easy it is to lose it. But the question still remains: How do we get and keep focus? How do we actually make the catch and score the touchdown?

To have focus, you need a very clear and narrowly defined objective. The importance of knowing where you're going cannot be overstated. Most peoples' lives are diluted by running in 17 directions. People are unaware that they've overspent themselves. And most don't even know where they're going in the first place!

Having focus also means you know what to say no to and how to say no often. You get the life you focus on. You get the results you focus on. The more you live and the more successful you become, the more the distractions you'll contend with to keep you from your goal. Your life's peripheral vision is full of shiny things that have nothing to do with your purpose or focus. Few people can avoid the distractions of the shiny thing. Most people are no better than the bass enticed by the shiny lure. It pulls them away from their reason for being and costs them their lives.

Successful people are rare because the ability to focus is rare. But focus is not impossible! When you overcome your fears, steer clear of greed, identify your objectives, and eliminate distractions, you're not only able to focus, you've set the stage for the next part of the equation—*I* for *Intensity*.

I for *Intensity*

Intensity has a lot to do with the degree of energy and determination you put forth. It's a decision. You can decide to what degree you're going to do something, even if it's difficult. Carelessly rolling out of bed every morning and arriving to work late is a very different decision than getting up every morning and attacking your work with the drive and mentality that you're unemployed—even when you've got a job!

Intensity is deciding to *bring it.* And *focused intensity* is deciding to *keep bringing it* over and over again. It's deciding to consistently maintain your attention and bring a high level of energy to something for more than eight freaking seconds! It's making intentional decisions and saying to yourself . . . *Starting right now and moving forward, I'm going to control my attitude and effort. Starting right now and moving forward, I'm going to be committed and trustworthy. Starting right now and moving forward, I'm going to work hard and put myself in position to make the catch and complete the play.*

Enthusiasm is a decision, a choice to be excited. Winston Churchill said, "Sucess is going from failure to failure without loss of enthusiasm." Creating and sustaining intensity doesn't happen by accident. It happens by making deliberate decisions every day that eventually become ingrained habits. It's reading and studying. It's taking care of your mind and body. It's growing and improving.

It's scribbling red marker in increments on a homemade paper thermometer taped to the refrigerator door to show how much debt you've paid off each month. Every colored inch represents all-in sacrifice and dedication to the goal. Every colored inch is extra money scraped together from a second or third job, or extra money saved from forfeiting summer vacations and meals out. All because getting rid of debt means freedom for you and your family to live the life you *want* to live—not the one you *have* to live. That's focused intensity! In fact, we even have a special name in our *Financial Peace University* teachings for this degree of focused intensity with money. We call it *gazelle intense*.

Gazelle Intense

The term *gazelle intense* came to me years ago in sort of an unlikely way. One day as I was studying what God says about money, I came across Proverbs 6:1 and 5: "If you become surety . . . deliver yourself like a gazelle from the hand of the hunter, and like a bird from the hand of the fowler" (NKJV). *Surety* is Bible talk for debt, so at first I thought this was just a cute little animal metaphor for getting out of debt. Then later that week I came across a show on the Discovery Channel about gazelles, and it completely changed my understanding. Gazelles are not cute—they're intense!

In this particular scene, a herd of gazelles was peacefully grazing on the African plains. Next, the camera panned to Mr. Cheetah sneaking up on them from the bushes. Suddenly the gazelles picked up a whiff of Mr. Cheetah and froze until he made his next move. In an instant, Mr. Cheetah leapt from the bushes and all the gazelles yelled to each other, "CHEEEETAAAAH! RUUUUNNNN!" At least that's what I imagined them yelling because they all ran for their lives every which way like it was a four-alarm fire . . . and poor Mr. Cheetah went home without lunch.

As I kept watching, I learned that the cheetah is the fastest mammal on dry land. Cheetahs can go from 0 to 45 miles per hour in four leaps. So how in the world do they only get a gazelle burger in 1 out of 19 chases?

The show went on to explain that the gazelle's survival tactic is to outmaneuver the cheetah as they run for their lives. In other words, gazelles scattering in 15 different directions isn't chaos, it's strategy. The cheetah gets overwhelmed and tires quickly. But keep in mind, he's only looking for lunch. The gazelles—they're fighting to live another day! Working toward a goal like your life depends on it . . . that's gazelle intense. That's how gazelles beat their primary hunter—which just happens to be the fastest mammal on land.

Likewise, that's how you beat debt and anything else that keeps you from the life you want to live. You have a plan and strategically run like your life depends on it!

Keep Bringing It

Now, it's obvious that gazelles only need to implement *gazelle intensity* in insolated moments of survival. At Ramsey, we use the metaphor specifically for people on Baby Steps 1-3 of the 7 Baby Steps. These people are getting out of debt and need a burst of do-or-die energy to overcome it. For some, they need to maintain this degree of intensity for six months. For others, three years. They apply gazelle intensity for however long it takes them to complete Baby Step 2 and get away from the thing that's threatening their life—debt.

With weight loss, this might look like you going all-out for three months with an intense workout program to lose 20 or 30 pounds. Then you'd keep the intensity applied so you don't slip backward. You'd make the daily choices to continue your new exercise and eating habits. Your health would become a top priority. You'd keep bringing the focus to this area of your life—and bringing it and bringing it and bringing it—until health and wellness became a lifestyle, not just an event.

That's *focused intensity*. It's making intentional choices and taking deliberate actions that keep constant pressure applied to your goals. It's consistently working to be better this year than you were last year. Year after year after year.

Which brings us to the next element in The Momentum Theorem: *T* for *Time*.

T for *Time*

Now I meet people all the time who can be focused and who can be intense, but I don't meet many who can do it over time—*Focused Intensity over Time*. Real momentum never happens quickly. It happens over a long period.

Ralph Waldo Emerson is often quoted for his famous saying: "You become what you think about." And this certainly speaks to the power of focus and intensity. But many of us don't realize that this is just part of the quote. Emerson's full quote is: "You become what you think about **all day long**." *Boom!* That's focused intensity *over Time*. It's the *all day long* part that makes the difference. Without time, focused intensity can't reach it's greatest impact.

Just imagine, then, what you could become when you turn up the focus and intensity on your goals from *all day long* to *all week long* . . .

From *all week long* to *all month long*.

From *all month long* to *all year long*.

From *all year long* to *all decade long*.

From *all decade long* to *all life long*.

Imagine what your business and leadership could look like! What your faith

and health and relationships could look like!

For example, when a new salesperson onboards at Ramsey Solutions, I always tell them, "If you'll go bananas for your first 90 days—just go crazy and spin up unbelievable levels of activity—you'll create so much momentum you'll eat off of it for the next two years. And the whole company will know your name!"

The same idea expands with longer periods of time. If you can have focused intensity on a certain task or subject for *a whole year*, you'll likely create such synergy in your life that everybody in your city or your industry will know your name and what you do. If you can keep focused intensity *over 10 years*, you might become a household name or at least a recognized expert and success in your space. You could begin to change the whole culture in your industry. And if you can stay on mission with focused intensity for *an entire career*, then you'll likely change the world in some major way and leave a lasting legacy.

The hard part is committing to the long haul. In his book *Outliers*, Malcolm Gladwell wrote, "Ten thousand hours is the magic number of greatness." But those 10,000 hours equate to *years* of effort and hard work, and sometimes years of trial and tribulation. Unfortunately, most people aren't willing to put in the painstaking hours to get great and stay great at something.

Perseverance

Sitting behind a microphone every day on *The Ramsey Show* doesn't make me the world's greatest broadcaster. But doing the show for three hours a day for decades? That's been the difference maker that's put us in the top two talk shows in the nation. Perseverance *over time*. It hasn't been easy. It hasn't been perfect. I just haven't quit. I've outlasted people that were supposed to be "the next biggest thing" in the radio industry. I've seen countless people much more talented than me come and go. They burst on the scene, start "trending," and then disappear. Why? Because they didn't have focused intensity *over time*.

As I've studied successful people over the years, I've found that there's a distinct correlation between perseverance and success. I know thousands of millionaires and decamillionaires, and I personally know at least 20 billionaires. Of those, one or two might be off-the-charts intelligent, but the majority don't have any unusual brilliance. As a matter of fact, Ramsey Solutions' *National Study of Millionaires* revealed that the typical millionaire has a college GPA below a 3.0. (Mine was a 2.97, and that .03 shortfall still ticks me off!) In other words, they're regular people except for one thing: they just don't quit. Their ability to persevere, to not be denied, to just keep after it, to push through anything and everything no matter how long it takes—that's what sets them apart.

Slow and Steady Wins the Race

One day, while I was having lunch with one of my billioinaire friends, I asked him how he's become so successful (a billion is a thousand million, by the way). He said his success is based on two things. The first is being generous. He's always made generosity a priority in his life. I knew him to be a generous man, so that wasn't too surpising to me. But the second thing he said shocked me at first, and even slightly disappointed me.

He said, "Dave, there's this book I read all the time."

All he had to say was "book" and I was excited! My life has been changed by reading books, so I couldn't wait to hear what his recommendation would be.

He continued, "This might be the most important book I've ever read other than the Bible."

Well, now I *really* wanted know what book he was talking about!

"Dave," he asked with a grin. "Have you ever read *The Tortoise and the Hare*?"

"Well, yes," I said. But I was thinking, *Ugh. You've got to be kidding, right? You're a billionaire and an uber-successful person in every area of your life, and your book recommendation is a children's fable?*

But then he went on to explain how this book's age-old message is significant for our culture today. He said that, sadly, we live in a world of immature people who can't stay focused and are always looking for a shortcut. He said that if people really want to stand out and be successful, they have to learn to stop looking for the shortest, quickest way to build relationships or do their work.

As he talked, I couldn't help but think that he was making the case for *focused intensity over time.*

He said, "Dave, I've read *The Tortoise and the Hare* over a thousand times, and every time I read it, the tortoise wins."

My brilliant billionaire friend couldn't be more right! On the outside, the tortoise isn't impressive in any way. But it doesn't matter. He's not concerned with how he looks or feels. He's not caught up in the emotion of the race or how much better the competition is or how hard the course seems. He brings his best game. He puts his focused intensity toward the finish line and doesn't stop. He just keeps walking. And walking. And walking. Until he wins.

Perseverance Produces Character

Perseverance wins—that's the good news. Perseverance helps us build muscles we don't even know we have. The bad news is, when you need perseverance, it means things are getting hard. But that's when hope kicks in! Romans 5:3–5 tells us that we can rejoice in our hard times because suffering produces perseverance, perseverance produces character, and character produces hope. And hope is what gets us through hard times.

People who know this better than anyone are our grandparents and great-grandparents who survived the Great Depression and World War II. There's a reason they're called "The Greatest Generation"! They learned how to hang on and fight through the longest, most severe economic downturn our country has ever seen. Then they rose up and took on Hitler to battle against the evils of genocide. They persevered. They never quit. And in doing so, they grew their character and their hope. They had a big enough *why*.

A Big Enough *Why*

My friend Simon Sinek has helped millions of people understand the power of having a huge *why* in his record-setting TedTalk and his book, *Start with Why*. When your *why*—your purpose for doing what you're doing—is big enough, it can drive you to persevere and work on something well beyond 10,000 hours. But if your *why* is only wrapped up in making money, building a brand, selling a product, or just keeping up with the Joneses, it will be too shallow and superficial to stand the test of time. Your *why* has to be deeper and more meaningful than that. It has to be about serving others—your customers, your spouse, your family, your community. Serving others is the only *why* strong enough to create and feed your focused intensity for a lifetime.

That's not to say that you won't get tired, scared, and overwhelmed by self-doubt along the way. You will. Doing meaningful work and sustaining meaningful relationships doesn't make you immune to the stress that can come with the responsibility and weight of it all. That's why it's important to have a big enough *why* and revisit it often.

At Ramsey we hold a company-wide staff meeting every Monday. That's more than a thousand team members in one room every week! We give updates on all the things that are happening in every business unit across the company. It's our way of letting the right hand know what the left hand is doing, so to speak. We of course show videos of the amazing events we've held and the national media clips that highlight our Ramsey Personalities, our teachings, and our products. We also give financial reports with arrows that usually point up.

But we also talk about hard things. Stressful things. Things that we try and fail at. Over the years we've talked about all kinds of mistakes we've made with lots of zeroes on the end. We've also talked about how we've failed each other. And how the lies spread about us in newspapers and social media hurt us but don't define us.

We share it all—the highlights and the lowlights. Our team could easily walk away from these meetings and feel like all we do is all about us. Except for one thing. We don't forget our *why*!

Every time we gather for staff meeting, we remind each other that we're blessed to be a blessing. And we make it a top priority to celebrate the heroes who've been impacted by our mission. We share story after story about the college graduate who finally made their last student loan payment . . . about the single mom who finally landed a higher-paying job with benefits for her kids . . . about the marriage that's been restored because the money fights have stopped. Our eyes leak as we cheer for hero after hero who's done the hard work and changed their lives because of a line of code we've written or a book we've shipped or an email we've sent. We don't ever leave that room without remembering our *why*.

Keeping your purpose at the front and center of everything you do helps you keep the highs and lows in perspective. It helps you remember that it's not about you—your worst day or your highlight reel. It's about persevering over time, showing up again and again for the people who need you. For as long as it takes.

G for God

Up to this point, the breakdown of The Momentum Theorem has been about everything *you* can bring to the equation. *You* can bring focus. *You* can bring intensity. *You* can commit to something over time. *You* can control all these things. You might even spin up some momentum on your own and reach some goals you've set. But they'll be outcomes you're expecting. Outcomes limited by you.

You see, you can plant corn and you can fertilize it. And you can hoe and keep the weeds out. But you don't get to control the sun. You don't get to control the rain. You don't get to decide the perfect combination for those two things to activate the DNA of that particular seed. You don't get to decide if this particular season will yield a bumper crop. You just don't get to decide. You do your part with the planting and the hoeing. God does His part with the sun and the rain.

Now, over the years I've run into lots of people who go to the extreme with their theology on this. They say, "I'm praying about it and waiting for God to show up." But I've often found that's really code for "I'm too dadgum lazy to do the work, so I'll just wait for God to do it all."

The Bible makes it very clear that we are to work hard and give our best effort. Verse after verse shows the cause-and-effect relationship between hard work and rewards, between laziness and ruin. At Ramsey, we believe this so wholeheartedly, we've made Colossians 3:23 one of our core values: "Whatever you do, work at it with all your heart, as working for the Lord" (NIV).

Here's the deal: If you plant nothing, the sun and the rain will create mud. In other words, you still need to show up and work! St. Ambrose said, "Work like it all depends on you, and pray like it all depends on God." So do the planting. Tend your fields. And pray.

Because you're not in charge of the sun or the rain. God is. You might not control what God chooses to do in His sovereignty, but you can ask Him to join you in the equation.

Now, hang with me here, because this is when things get fun! You see, I'm a math nerd. I love calculus. It's the only place we humans get to play with infinity. And if you understand how infinity works, you know that any time you multiply anything by the infinite, you get an infinite answer on the other side of the equals sign. It's an amazing concept on its own. But when you apply the concept to The Momentum Theorem, it's mindblowing! Even if you're not a math nerd and would rather lick a cheese grater than do calculus, this should excite you!

Why?

Because God is infinite. And we humans aren't. We're incurably finite. Limited. Stoppable. But God? He's infinite. Unlimited. Unstoppable.

Think about the implications of that. The God of the universe, who created us, who wants a relationship with us, who wants to be a part of every aspect of our lives, is infinite and unstoppable. That means, anything multiplied by Him is unstoppable.

Luke 18:27 tells us, "What is impossible with man is possible with God" (NIV). So why wouldn't we want to work hard and bring our part of the equation—our *focused intensity over time*—to the God of all things possible? Why wouldn't we seek for Him to multiply our efforts by His immeasurable power? Why wouldn't we pray and ask Him to complete our equation with the unstoppable momentum only He can bring?

If we invite Him into our equation, God can play a big part in our story. We can't create unstoppable momentum without Him. We're not meant too. It's not supposed to be all up to us. We need Him in order to be complete. Otherwise, we can't have balance in our work, our marriage, our parenting, or our relationships.

Work Like It All Depends On You, Pray Like It All Depends On God

I've kept a prayer journal since the early 1990s. Remember, that's when I was fresh out of my bankruptcy trench. I had met God on the way up to my first million, but I got to know Him on the way down. I learned about His grace and peace and love. I learned about His sovereignty and His plan and purposes for my life. I came to know the promise of Jeremiah 29:11: "'For I know the plans I have for you,' declares the LORD, 'plans to prosper you, and not to harm you, plans to give you hope and a future'" (NIV).

It's interesting to look back through my journal and see the prayers and goals I wrote down and reflect on how God did or didn't answer them through the years. An entry from 1994 shows the goals I jotted about my radio show, my *Financial Peace* book, and the *Financial Peace University* class I was teaching . . .

By the end of 1995, I want to:
- Grow the radio show from 1 city to 25 cities.
- Sell 50,000 *Financial Peace* books. [At the time, I had sold 6,000 out of the trunk of my car.]

- Teach *Financial Peace University* classes in 5 cities. [At the time, I was teaching in just one city, wearing a bad suit, and using an overhead projector in an uninspiring hotel room.]

By the end of 1995, I had missed every one of these goals. The radio show was still in one city, I had sold only 37,000 *Financial Peace* books, and *Financial Peace University* was only in three cities.

Again, I prayed and set goals to hit . . .

By the end of 1996, I want to:
- Grow the radio show to 75 cities.
- Sell 200,000 *Financial Peace* books.
- Teach *Financial Peace University* in 25 cities.

Again, I missed every one of them. The radio show grew to 12 cities, not 75. We sold 110,000 *Financial Peace* books, not 200,000. *Financial Peace University* still remained in three cities, not 25.

But looking back, these weren't misses at all. These were goals with work boots on. The team and I had *focused intensity* and were taking action *over time*, year after year. We were intentionally planting seeds in the ground to produce fruit. We applied constant pressure to the things we wanted to see move. And we prayed. For God's guidance and wisdom. For vision and clarity. For grace and blessing. For Him to do what only He can do. For His will, His plans, His timing—not ours.

Today, I'm writing this book at the end of 2021. And it blows my freaking mind that . . .

At the end of this year, we've:

- Reached 23 million people weekly with our radio shows, podcasts, and videos.
- Published 19 bestselling books, including 3 million copies of *Financial Peace*.
- Reached nearly 10 million people with our guided money plan, including *Financial Peace University* in more than 50,000 churches.

These things didn't magically happen because I wrote them down or wished for them. They didn't happen because I'm faster, smarter, better-looking, or had any kind of special privilege. They didn't happen because God loves me more—or less. They didn't happen because I worked hard and did it all on my own. They didn't happen because I sat back in my easy chair and let God do all the work.

All these things have happened because I've put The Momentum Theorem in play in my life for more than 30 years . . .

$$Fi/T(G) = M$$

Focused Intensity, over Time, multiplied by God,
equals Unstoppable Momentum.

Conclusion

Thirty years ago, I could have easily believed what the debt collector told my wife . . . *Loser.*

I was beat up enough to believe it. Lord knows I was scared enough. I was a 28-year-old husband and father of a brand-new baby and a toddler—and I was bankrupt. I'd lost it all, and it put me and my young family in a dark place.

Remember, if you don't have momentum, you look dumber and worse than you really are. The darkness clouds your vision—and the vision of those around you.

But there's something interesting about the darkness. If you don't choose to lay down in it and shut your eyes, it can cause you to search for the light.

Think about it. When you walk into a dark room, what's the first thing you reach for? The light switch, right? Even if you're bruised, broken, and scared, you still look for a way to turn on a light so you can see better. Darkness causes us to take action. To flip a switch. To strike a match. To light a fire. It causes us to get focused and push the darkness back with a greater level of intensity.

Sure, I had made mistakes. But I had also made a million dollars. I knew making a million could be done. And once you know something can be done, you can do it again—better. With momentum. With *focused intensity, over time, multiplied by God*.

If I hadn't gone bankrupt, I would've just been a guy who owned some real estate. And that would've been a good life. But instead, God changed the trajectory of my life to have a whole lot more meaning—a bigger *why*—than I'd been on track to have. Without Him, I was just going to be a collector of stuff. Now I'm a collector of stories. Stories like yours.

Like I said at the beginning of this book, The Momentum Theorem isn't exclusive to my story. It's meant for you and your story too. You might be slogging in a dark trench right now, looking dumber and worse than you really are. Or you might be in an unexplainable swirl of something that resembles Oprah's magic dust, looking smarter and better than you are. Either way, you've now got a new lens to see through. The elements of The Momentum Theorem can help you cut through the darkness and the dust and give you (and others) a more accurate way to see where you are and where you're going.

So take a moment and lift your head out of the dark and/or the dust. Look back over the past year or five years. Can you see where you've had focus? Can you see specific things that are beginning to break loose and move forward because of the pressure and intensity you're applying to them? Can you see where God has shown up and answered prayers in unexpected ways?

If you can't, what parts are missing? The *focused intensity* part? The *over time* part? The *multiplied by God* part? Maybe you feel like you're missing all the parts of the theorem in your story and the whole thing needs a rewrite.

The great news is: It's your story. You can shift gears in any area of your life at any time. Your can turn the dial in your business, leadership, marriage, parenting, health, finances, and faith. You can determine to what extent you will bring intensity and perseverance to all these things.

You can spend more time with your spouse and kids. You can prioritize your health. You can budget and plan for your financial future. You can pour into your team and push initiatives at work. You can commit to all these things for the long haul.

Most importantly, you can pray and invite God in. And when you do—when things start breaking wide open beyond all you could ever ask or imagine—you won't be surprised at all.

You'll smile, brush the dirt and dust from your eyes, and know exactly what to call it. *Unstoppable Momentum.*

Bonus Material

Goal-Setting Guide

As you saw from my story, part of getting focused and building intensity to create unstoppable momentum is to get clear on your goals. Goals are dreams with work boots on. It's good to have dreams, but you need a way to activate them. Without goals, dreams can tend to be someday wishes, like . . . *I wish I could be a millionaire someday.* But wishes are -ish. And just -ishing your way along won't cut it. If you -ish it, you'll get -ish results. Goals take the -ish out of wishing. Goals pull your dreams out of the clouds and make them tangible and achievable.

So first, you need to identify your dreams. Consider the seven key areas of your life and determine what your dreams are in each area:

- Career
- Financial
- Spiritual
- Physical

- Intellectual
- Family
- Social

What do you envision for your business, leadership, marriage, parenting, friendships, health, finances, and faith? Take some time to dream, and then write down your dreams for each category. This will show you where you ultimately want to end up.

Next comes the exciting, take-action part: goal-setting. Once you've identified your dreams, you'll need to determine the steps to take to get where you want to be. Goal-setting will help you do just that. The following framework outlines the five essential elements of goal-setting. As you apply these elements, you'll find that they'll not only activate your dreams, they'll also activate unstoppable momentum in all areas of your life.

5 Essential Goal-Setting Guidelines

1. Goals must be specific.

Vagueness is the archenemy of goal-setting and will only cause you to feel overwhelmed and give up. Get clear about your goals and the actions you need to take in order to make them happen. Ask yourself, *What exactly am I trying to accomplish here? When and why do I want to achieve this goal? Who does my goal involve? What has to be true that's not true today?* For instance, what has to be true in your financial situation to become debt-free or to start investing? What has to be true for you to lead your team better? What has to be true for you to grow in your faith this year? Whatever it is, get clear and be specific.

2. Goals must be measurable.

In order to know if you've achieved your goal, you need to be able to measure it. How will you know when you've reached it? For example, if you want to lose weight, you wouldn't just write down "lose weight" as a goal. You'd need to specify how many pounds you want to lose or what favorite jeans you want to fit in again. Your ability to button those jeans and still breathe would make that goal measurable. Maybe you're focused on saving money for your kid's college fund. "Save for college" is not measurable, but "save $75,000 for Junior to go to my alma mater" is measurable.

3. Goals must have a time limit.

Time limits are important in goal-setting because they give us a finish line. And finish lines help us, well, finish. Giving yourself a time frame can also help you set realistic goals and even stretch yourself a little. Once you take a specific, measurable goal and put a time limit on it, the math of the progress naturally appears.

Let's say you want to lose 30 pounds. When? (If you're like me, maybe the more realistic question is: How many times do you want to lose 30 pounds?) Put a reasonable time limit on it and watch what happens: "Lose 30 pounds in three months." Now that's a measurable, specific goal with a time limit! Thirty pounds over three months is 10 pounds a month or two and a half pounds a week. Breaking it down like this, you'll be able to tell how you're doing every week.

Maybe you want to make $100,000. Great! When? If you'd like to make that much in one year, well then, now you've got a goal! Making $100,000 a year works out to $8,333 per month or around $2,100 a week. The math makes it measurable and takes you from dreamer to goal-setter.

Want to read 12 leadership books in the next 12 months? Create a reading plan that includes how many pages you'll need to read daily, weekly, and monthly in order to reach your goal. As you go, you might find that you can stretch yourself and read more books throughout the year. Setting and meeting time limits will give you a baseline for how much you can achieve. This also grows your capacity for reaching bigger goals in the future.

4. Goals must be *your* goals.

Only *you* can set your goals because only *you* can set your heart and mind. Your goals shouldn't be your friend's, your spouse's, your parents' or your pastor's goals for you. "My wife wants me to lose weight" is not *your* goal, it is *her* wish.

And your goals certainly shouldn't be my goals for you! You see, I can teach you the 7 Baby Steps, but I can't make, save, and invest your money for you. If you want to be debt-free and become a millionaire, *you've* got to be the one to pay off debt, save, and invest in order to reach those milestones. Take it from me, the victory is much sweeter when you're the hero of your own story. And of course, if you're married, you and your spouse need to align and pull in the same direction. But whether you're single or married, taking ownership of your goals will ensure that you make the necessary choices and adjustments in your life to make them happen.

5. Goals must be in writing.

Successful people live intentionally. They put their goals in writing—on paper, on purpose. Habakkuk 2:2 tells us, "Write the vision, and make it plain" (ASV). Writing down your dreams and setting specific goals around those dreams makes your vision plain. It gives you clarity so that you know you're not climbing a ladder that's leaning against the wrong building. Written goals give you a way to take action on your aspirations, track your progress, and stay motivated. Most of all, this practice helps you impose your will on your life versus just letting life happen to you.

Proverbs 29:18 tells us: "Where there is no vision, the people perish" (KJV). In my noble hillbilly heritage, to me this reads: *If we're not dreaming and setting goals, we might just as well be roadkill.* Andy Dufresne put it this way in the movie *Shawshank Redemption*: "Get busy living or get busy dying." In order to make the most out of this life we've been given, we all need to get clear about our dreams and the goals that will make them a reality. We need to get focused so that we can get about the business of reaching our goals.

The five essential goal-setting guidelines I've laid out will help you be intentional and go after the goals that stand between you and

Unstoppable Momentum. Following this framework, you'll be well on your way to building focused intensity in all areas of your life. It's game on, baby!

NOTES

1. Statistic Brain, "Attention Span Statistics," Statistic Brain Research Institute (March 2, 2018): https://www.statisticbrain.com /attention-span-statistics/, quoted in Alyson Gausby, "Microsoft Attention Spans Research Report," Consumer Insights, Microsoft Canada (Spring 2015): https://www.scribd.com/document/265348695/Microsoft -Attention-Spans-Research-Report.

2. Rob Arthur, "The Shrinking Shelf Life of NFL Players," *The Wall Street Journal*, updated February 29, 2016, https://www.wsj.com/articles /the-shrinking-shelf-life-of-nfl-players-1456694959.

3. Pablo S. Torre, "How (and Why) Athletes Go Broke," *Sports Illustrated Vault*, March 23, 2009, https://vault.si.com/vault/2009/03/23/how -and-why-athletes-go-broke.

4. Greg Bishop, "Taking Vows in a League Blindsided by Divorce," *The New York Times*, August 8, 2009, https://www.nytimes.com/2009/08/09 /sports/football/09marriage.html.

ABOUT THE AUTHOR

 **DAVE RAMSEY** is America's trusted voice on money and business. He's a #1 national bestselling author and host of *The Ramsey Show*, heard by more than 18 million listeners each week. Dave's eight national bestselling books include *The Total Money Makeover*, *Baby Steps Millionaires*, and *EntreLeadership*. Since 1992, Dave has helped people take control of their money, build wealth, and enhance their lives. He also serves as CEO of Ramsey Solutions.